TRAVEL 1
DOGS AN

David Prydie BVMS, CertSAO, MRCVS
Cartoons by Russell Jones

INSTINCTIVELY • CATS AND DOGS

Published by
Instinctively Cats and Dogs
The Seedbed Centre
Langston Road
Loughton
Essex
IG10 1SW

Telephone 0208 502 4487
Fax 0208 508 5782

through
Ringpress Books Ltd, Lydney, Gloucs

First edition 1999
© David Prydie (text) Russell Jones (illustrations)

ISBN 1 86054 118 6

Designed by Rob Benson

Printed in Malta through Printworks International Ltd

TRAVEL TIPS FOR DOGS AND CATS

This book is dedicated to all those pet owners who choose their house and car with their pets in mind. Now they have the chance to choose their holiday destination in the same way.

PREFACE

About the author:
David Prydie BVMS, CertSAO, MRCVS.

The son of a vet, David graduated from Glasgow Veterinary School in 1981 and has an additional qualification in orthopaedics in dogs and cats. He has more than eighteen years' experience as a vet in England, Scotland and Wales. He currently works in a state-of-the-art pet practice in North London. With his fiancée (a former veterinary nurse) he has recently set up a company to promote people's enjoyment of their pets. He lives with seven cats and one dog (all rescues) and travels everywhere with the dog and sometimes the cats. The family group has moved house four times in the past year!

TRAVEL TIPS FOR YOUR DOG AND CAT

CONTENTS

INTRODUCTION

Pets are very much a part of the family today. People often select their house (near dog walks, away from busy roads) and cars (estate or hatchback) with their pets in mind. Similarly, many people choose to take holidays in the UK rather than be separated from their pets. With the changes to quarantine rules for the UK, taking pets on holiday outside the UK will become commonplace.

Many hotels in UK now accept pets in the bedrooms. This trend is likely to increase, especially if the hotels want to attract the foreign visitor who is used to his or her pet accompanying them.

A NOTE ABOUT RABIES

Rabies was spread from Eastern Europe to the West via foxes following First World War trenches. A successful vaccination regime has seen the disease decline to its present low levels. The traditional notion of a mad, foaming dog is the terminal stages of the disease, which takes several months to devlop. Rabies can only be transmitted via a bite from an infected animal. The significant early signs are changes in character and behaviour. The obvious way to avoid rabies is to keep yourself and your pet away from any strange animal.

BEFORE YOU GO

TAKE A GOOD LOOK AT YOUR PET

Assess your pet's ability to travel and be honest with yourself. If your dog is ill or in poor health, recovering from surgery or pregnant, consider postponing the trip or arranging someone to look after your pet. For example, have your pet stay with a neighbour or friend, or put your dog in reputable kennels, or arrange for a pet sitter.

If your pet has not travelled before, it is worth starting with shorter journeys.

DOES YOUR PET NEED TO GO TO THE VET?

If your pet is on medication, make sure you have sufficient supplies to last not only for the journey, but also while you are away.

Make sure your pet's vaccinations are up to date. While diseases such as parvo and distemper are less commonly seen in some areas, they are still rife in others. Allow sufficient time for vaccinations to take effect. Most vaccinations require an initial course of two injections two to three weeks apart, with a booster given annually. Don't leave it until the last minute to check on your pet's vaccination status, as there may be insufficient time to complete a course if the boosters have lapsed. Also, after its inoculation it is quite normal for an animal to be slightly dull for a day or two – this is not a good time for your pet to travel. Leaving enough time for vaccinations will be especially relevant once the new rabies laws come into force.

Fleas and ticks can be a big problem in warmer climates. It is best to treat your pet before leaving. Most of the newer products last at least a month. Ask your vet for advice.

Clip your pet's nails if needed and give him a good brush to try to reduce the amount of hair shed during the journey.

A CURRENT IDENTITY TAG OR MICROCHIP

Check your dog has an up-to-date identity disc or even consider having your dog microchipped in case of loss. A small microchip can be implanted painlessly in your pet's neck. This microchip can be read by a scanner and most vets, rescue centres and some police stations have these. Your pet's unique number is recorded on a national database, identifying you as the owner. If you wish to take your pet abroad once the rabies laws change, a microchip will be compulsory.

WHAT TO TAKE

Take a spare lead and collar, a suitable bed and cover for the car and/or hotel room.

Ensure that you have enough food and water for the journey as well as suitable bowls. Very neat and compact travelling sets are now available.

If your pet is on a special diet, or is used to one particular brand of food, ensure that you have sufficient to last the duration of your stay. Your pet's specific food may be difficult to obtain outside the UK.

TRAVELLING BY
CAR

DOGS

Position your dogs in the car so as not to cause accidents, and to prevent them injuring themselves or you in an accident. In estate cars or hatchbacks the use of travelling kennels or a dog guard is to be recommended, as it will stop the dog from being catapulted forward in the event of sudden braking. For dogs travelling on the back seats the use of a seatbelt retainer is advised. These attach to the normal seatbelt attachment and hold the dog firm in the event of sudden braking. Dogs should not travel in a position where it is possible for them to interfere with either the driver or the controls.

START THEM YOUNG

Most puppies are carsick, but it is important to persevere with car journeys, as most will outgrow this trait. Start by trying to reduce the amount of excitement. Put them in the car for short periods – for instance when washing it – but do not go anywhere. When the dog is comfortable being in the car, start the engine and leave it running for a short period with the dog still in the car. Finally, start with short journeys and then graduate to longer ones. Try to take the dog in the car on a variety of occasions – not just to the vet. For fractious dogs, a travelling cage is essential.

VENTILATION

Ventilation on a journey is important. Dogs can only sweat from their pads and nose. They lose heat by radiating it and by panting. *They are far less tolerant of heat than people*. It is therefore important to have some form of ventilation in the car. Do not let your dog hang out of the window. In this situation you are not in control of the dog and he may be a danger to other road users. Furthermore, dogs hanging their heads out of the window will suffer from drying of the eyes, causing what is called exposure conjunctivitis.

Remember the effect of the sun beating down on a large rear window. You may be reasonably comfortable sat in the front of the car, but your dog may be subjected to the direct heat of the sun. Consider using car window blinds. Do not leave dogs in cars unattended.

WATER

Always carry water when travelling with your dog. Stop at least every 2 hours and allow your dog to go to the toilet, stretch his legs and have a drink. Rather neat travelling bowls and utility belts are now available. In hot weather these stops may need to be more frequent. In especially hot weather consider travelling in the early morning or late evening.

FEEDING

Give your dog only a light meal before travelling. If the journey is particularly long, this can be supplemented by small snacks during the journey. Always provide water.

Heat stroke – see Emergencies (Page 55).

DRUGS

Despite familiarisation with travelling in the car, some dogs still suffer travel sickness or get over-excited. Certain medications may help these animals. It is important that the vet checks your pet before prescribing these, as some will affect other medical conditions, such as heart disease and epilepsy.

ACP – acepromazine – is the most commonly prescribed travel sedative for dogs. It is a very strong sedative, so expect a wobbly, drunk-looking dog. Tablets are given about half to one hour before travelling. Effects last 8 hours or more. Not suitable for dogs with heart disease or epilepsy.

Valium-Diazepam has variable effects, but, when combined with propanalol, works well on fractious dogs. Valium works reasonably well on cats. Animals are not so sedated as with ACP but are more relaxed. Effects last for only a few hours.

Emmiquel Metoclopramide is an anti-emetic. Particularly useful on dogs that are prone to vomiting. Tablets are given about half to one hour before travelling. No sedative effects, hence little or no effect on the fractious animal.

CATS

For cats travelling anywhere, a suitable, sturdy carrier is essential. A cardboard box is not acceptable. There should be sufficient room for the cat to lie down and turn round. The cat should feel safe and be able to see out. A range of suitable cages is available from most pet shops. Never travel with the cat free in the car or with someone holding the cat.

The cage should be positioned in the car in such a way that the cat can see out and that there is room for air to circulate around the box. Avoid placing the box in direct sun and try to provide some sort of shading. Cats can suffer from heat stroke in the same way as dogs. Do not leave cats in cars unattended.

If your cat messes when travelling, or if you are going on a longer journey, consider putting a litter tray with absorbent material in the bottom of the carrier and then remove it if soiled, allowing your cat to stay clean during the remainder of the journey. When you open the carrier make sure your cat cannot escape from the car. Do not open the carrier at any other time during the journey.

WATER

On longer journeys a bowl with water should be provided. Most modern carriers come with dishes attached to the wire door. The water should be topped up

during longer journeys without opening the carrier.
Consider using an athlete's drinks bottle with straw
attachment.

FEEDING

Feed only a small meal before travelling. If your cat is
prone to travel sickness then this can be omitted, but
ensure water is available.

TRAVELLING BY
TRAIN

Most train companies will accept pets, provided they are accompanied, but some may require them to travel in the guard's van. This will certainly be the case if they are unaccompanied. It is best to check with the individual company before booking. Dogs are even allowed on the London underground, but have to be carried on the escalators.

DOGS

As with all journeys, a bit of forethought will be required. Make sure your dog has been to the toilet before boarding the train. Make provision for water and food on the journey. Try to pick a time when the train is likely to be less busy. Small dogs will be all right sitting on their owner's lap but big dogs should not be allowed to sit on the seats. If the journey is very long, consider breaking it – even for an hour – then catching the next connecting train. Make sure your dog is clean, as this is less likely to provoke complaints from other travellers. Consider having him bathed and groomed or clipped before the journey

CATS

Cats are usually OK on trains but should always be in a suitable cage. As with travelling in a car, a litter tray in the bottom of the cage that can be easily changed during the journey is a good idea and the best way of getting rid of smells that may annoy other travellers. On no account should you let your cat out of the cage until you have arrived at your destination.

TRAVELLING BY
BOAT

YACHTS, CRUISERS AND CANAL BOATS

Both dogs and cats can swim but may find it difficult to walk on a smooth deck surface. Introduce your dog to this gradually, letting him get used to the pitch and roll of he boat. Most dogs gain their sea legs quickly. Obviously for longer journeys toilet stops will be required. If you are going out to sea, a dog life jacket is good idea.

FERRIES

Here the dog or cat may be in a car or may be taken on board by a foot passenger. If the dog or cat is travelling in your car then the same rules will apply as for transporting by car. Some ferry companies require pets to stay in the car during the crossing, and will only accept them on this basis. If during the crossing, the car is below decks where it is cool, consider leaving the window down only a little way to prevent too many fumes getting into the car. If the temperature where the dog is going to be is warm or in direct sun light, insist that the dog be allowed on deck with you; failing this, shade the car and arrange for a fan which can plug into the cigarette lighter.

TRAVEL TIPS FOR DOGS AND CATS

Animals accompanying foot passengers should be under control at all times. For cats this means being in a suitable cage throughout the journey. Dogs must be kept on a lead at all times. Although they may be allowed on deck, they will not be allowed in the cafeterias and will not be allowed on seats. Make sure they have been to the toilet before boarding.

CRUISE LINERS

Some cruise liners – such as the QE II – accept dogs. Dogs have their own attendant appointed and a special toilet area on board. With this sort of travel it is essential to check with the company before booking.

Pay particular attention to your dog's existing health conditions. If your pet has heart trouble then flying is not advised. Certain short-nosed breeds, such as Bulldogs, are more susceptible to breathing difficulties, and flying may make these worse. Check with your vet.
Pets must be over 8 weeks of age to fly, but leaving it until the animal is at least 12 weeks old may be better.

GET YOUR PET CHECKED BY YOUR VET

It is important to check if your animal is in a fit condition to fly. Although he or she may appear normal, there may be an undetected heart condition which would be made worse by flying. Some airlines require a health certificate before accepting pets. Check with the airline if this is required and how long before flying the health certificate has to be completed. Check you have all the necessary documentation before leaving, especially if you are going to a foreign country.

CARRIERS/CAGES

If your animal is going to travel in a carrier then make sure you have a sturdy, well-ventilated crate of adequate size. Your pet must be able to stand up, turn round and lie down comfortably. There should be a rim protruding at least 2 centimetres to prevent air holes from being obstructed. The interior should be free of potentially dangerous protrusions and the crate must have a door that fastens securely. It should be possible to pick the crate up without the risk of being bitten. The base should be leak-proof and covered with a towel or absorbent material. All carriers/cages must conform to the international standard regulated by IATA. Airlines may refuses to accept pets if the carriers they are presented in fail to meet these standards. A list of suppliers of airline approved carriers is given on Page 74.

Air Pets Oceanic, located near Heathrow, is a company specialising in the export and transportation of pets that offers a comprehensive service. The address is given on Page 74.

CONSIDER YOUR FLIGHT OPTIONS

Not all airlines accept pets, so check before booking. Avoid weekends or peak holiday periods and other times when delays are likely. Always travel on scheduled flights, as these are less likely to be delayed. Try to use only direct flights, as this cuts down the flying time and the possibility of things going wrong.

Avoid flying in very cold or very hot times of year, remembering what the conditions may be like at your destination.

Although some airlines may permit small dogs or cats in the cabin as hand luggage, most will require pets to travel in the hold. If they are accompanied, they will go as excess baggage; cargo if unaccompanied.

CHECK-IN

You will have to make a reservation for your pet to fly and this must be done when booking your own flights. The airline will advise you of arrangements at the airport, but allow for at least an extra two hours for check-in.

Ensure that the carrier your pet is travelling in is marked on all sides with large lettering "LIVE ANIMAL" with an arrow pointing up. Also record clearly on the carrier your name, address, contact phone number (both at home and at destination), destination and flight number.

Give about half your pet's normal food ration and water two to four hours before departure. Provide empty food and water dishes secured inside the carrier which can be filled from outside without opening the carrier. Attach food and water to the outside of the carrier with a 24-hour history of feeding and watering. Also attach a lead to the outside of the carrier. Do not include toys in the crate as these may cause choking, but an article of clothing from yourself may help your pet to settle, as it will carry your scent.

Only one adult animal, or two puppies or two kittens under six months per carrier is permitted.

When boarding the plane ask the cabin crew to confirm your pet has been loaded.

DRUGS

Most sedatives, such as ACP, would not be recommended as they cause a significant drop in blood pressure, which may be hazardous when flying. For the very fractious animal, diazepam may be used.

DELAYS AND STOPS

If your flight is delayed for any length of time, ask to see your pet. If it has already been loaded in the hold, ask the captain to check on the hold temperature.

If the plane has a stopover, ask to have your pet unloaded and then reloaded nearer to take-off, especially if the outside temperature is high. If you have a connecting flight or have to change planes, always claim your pet and then recheck him or her in again. Never check your pet through to the final destination in these circumstances.

CLAIMING YOUR PET

Claim your pet as soon as possible. Most pet carriers will be brought out to the baggage reclaim area. Occasionally, however, your pet may end up on the baggage carousel, so be sure to check with ground staff where your pet will emerge.

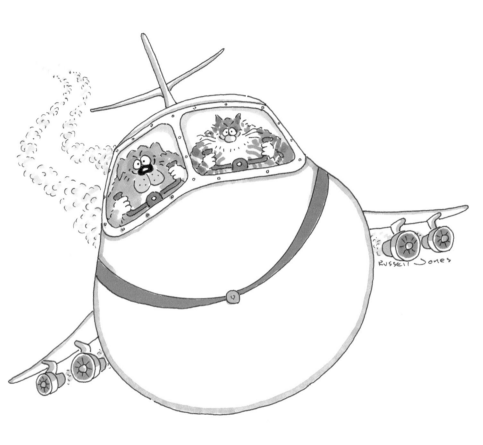

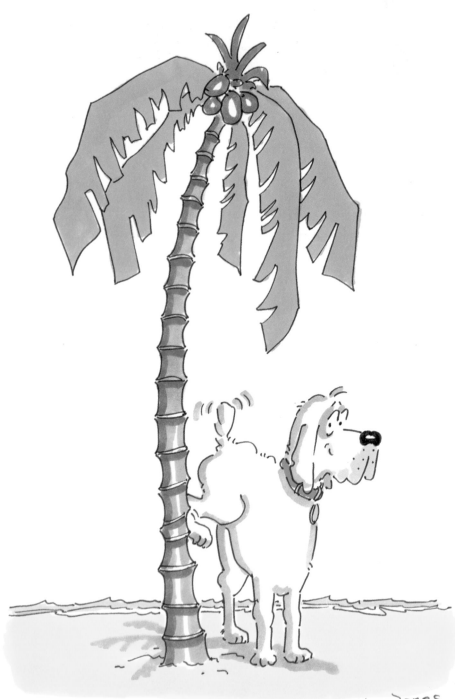

RUSSELL JONES.

TAKING YOUR PET
ABROAD

The rabies laws in the UK change from April 2000. From then it will be possible for animals to enter the UK without having to undergo six months of quarantine, provided they meet strict criteria, details of which are given in the next section, Rabies Update.

If you are taking your pet to a foreign country, a health certificate may be required. For some countries this can be issued up to 30 days before entry, others require it to have been issued within the preceding seven days and some countries do not require a certificate at all. It is best to check with MAFF (the Ministry of Agriculture, Fisheries and Food – see Page 73) or the embassy of the country concerned. Certain other requirements will have to be met for some countries. For instance, Australia requires dogs to be blood-sampled for Leptospirosis and Brucellosis. These samples can be taken by your vet, but remember to allow sufficient time for the laboratory to process the samples. There will be a specified time when such samples will need to be taken. Similarly, certain countries insist that worming and insecticidal treatments are carried out by a vet prior to departure. Rabies vaccination is required by some countries, and this and other criteria will have to be met if you wish to bring your pet back into the UK.

RABIES UPDATE

THE PET TRAVEL SCHEME (PETS)

The British government has announced details of the PET TRAVEL SCHEME. A pilot scheme will commence in April 2000, with the main scheme starting in 2001.

Quarantine is not being abolished completely. The new system will allow cats and dogs meeting certain conditions to enter the UK without having to go into quarantine.

The conditions of the scheme are as follows:

The pilot scheme:

- Only applies to cats and dogs
- Is limited to cats and dogs coming from the following countries: Andorra, Austria, Belgium, Denmark, Finland, France, Germany, Gibraltar, Greece, Iceland, Italy, Liechtenstein, Luxembourg, Monaco, Netherlands, Norway, Portugal, San Marino, Spain, Sweden, Switzerland, Vatican
- Will only operate on certain sea, air and rail routes to the UK.

Cats and dogs entering the UK must be fitted with a permanent number microchip, have been vaccinated against rabies using an approved vaccine (and have a booster vaccination at the required intervals), and have been blood-tested at a laboratory recognised by MAFF to show required immunity (antibodies level) has been achieved after vaccination.

Animals may not be brought into the UK from abroad until at least six months after the blood tests.

Up to April 2000, animals resident in the UK that are microchipped, vaccinated and blood-sampled prior to the date that the pilot scheme becomes operational will not have to wait six months from the date of the successful blood test before coming back to the UK after a trip abroad. After the date the pilot scheme becomes operational, animals will not be able to return to the UK until 6 months after a successful blood test.

Animals must be accompanied by a health certificate signed by an official veterinary surgeon (LVI) certifying that the above requirements have been met. These certificates will be available prior to the scheme going live. Animals must have been treated for certain parasites (the fox tapeworm *Echinococcus multilocularis*) and ticks. This should be done 24-48 hours before the pet enters the UK. The pet should be accompanied by a certificate signed by an official vet, certifying that these treatments have been given.

Transport companies allowed to transport pets will be approved by MAFF and be subject to regular auditing. A list of companies is not available at present. Before the pet enters the UK on one of the pilot scheme routes, its microchip, health certificate of rabies vaccination and certificate of treatment against certain parasites will be checked by the transport company. There will also be MAFF spot checks. Pets who do not pass inspection will have to go into quarantine on return to the UK, or in the case of pets from outside the UK, return to their own country. It is therefore essential that pet owners check that their pets meet the conditions of the scheme before they travel to the UK. For pet owners leaving the UK to return later, it is advised that they check that their pet meets the conditions of the scheme before they leave, otherwise it may be refused entry or have to go into quarantine when it arrives back in the UK.

WHAT PET OWNERS SHOULD DO NOW

Pet owners wishing to travel to a qualifying country after April 2000 should have their pet microchipped and vaccinated against rabies now, and then blood-tested. The MAFF advice is that the blood test should be done approximately 30 days after the rabies vaccine. The animal must be microchipped before it is vaccinated and blood-tested.

For the pilot scheme, a blood test is only required after the first vaccination (if successful), provided the pet has been re-vaccinated (booster vaccinated) at the intervals specified by the vaccine manufacturer. If there is a break in the specified vaccination programme, a further blood test will be required after re-vaccination. The blood test has to be sent to an approved laboratory. Currently, there are only two in the UK but more will follow. Greendale laboratories are quoting a turn-round time of 2 weeks for results.

ROUTES

The routes are expected to include the Calais to Dover sea crossings, Eurotunnel Shuttle Services, certain sea routes into Portsmouth from France, and certain air routes into Heathrow from Europe. These routes are not yet confirmed and it is too early for pet owners to book a ticket to travel with their pet.

TAKING YOUR PET TO
FRANCE

If you want to take your pet with you to France and then bring him or her back into Great Britain at the end of your stay, you will have to do the following:

1. Get your pet microchipped.

2. Get your pet vaccinated against rabies.

3. Get your pet blood-sampled to show the rabies vaccination has worked. This sample will have to be taken 30 days after the vaccination.

If you do the above before April 2000, your pet will be able to travel immediately after April 2000.

If the above is done after April 2000, you will have to wait 6 months after the blood test before your pet will be eligible to travel.

4. Make sure your pet's other vaccinations are up to date. The French authorities recommend that dogs are vaccinated against distemper, hepatitis and parvovirus at least 30 days – but no more than 12 months – before entering France.

Cats are recommended to be vaccinated against Infectious leucopaenia (enteritis.) Again, this must be at least 30 days – but no more than 12 months – before entering France.

5. Contact MAFF
   Animal Health (International Trade) Division B
   Hook Rise South
   Tolworth
   Surbiton
   Surrey KT6 7NT
   Tel:- 020 8330 8184

Request the bilingual certificate for export of dogs and cats to France.

6. Check that your vet is an appointed LVI (Local Veterinary Inspector.) If not, find one that is.

Take the bilingual certificate to the LVI. Get him or her to complete and sign the form. This must be done within 10 days of travelling.

7. Other points
   All cats and dogs must be over 3 months of age.

A maximum of three animals may be brought in, one of which can be a puppy (3-6 months old.)

Dogs and cats not intended for sale must be accompanied or met at the port of entry.

8. Dogs and cats for sale or for competition

a) No restriction on numbers.
b) All animals must be over 3 months old.
c) Bilingual export health certificate, as above.
d) Distemper, parvo and hepatitis vaccination
   recommended for dogs, and feline enteritis for cats.
e) Prior authorisation (health derogation) which is
   obtained from
   Direction de la Qualite
   Bureau des Exchanges Internationaux
   175 rue de Chevaleret
   75646 Paris
   Cedex 13
f) Animals intended for sale can only enter through certain
   ports and may be subjected to a health inspection at the
   customs office of entry.

BRINGING YOUR PET BACK FROM FRANCE

Provided you complied with the microchipping, rabies
vaccination and blood-testing before you left, your pet will
be allowed back into Britain without having to go into
quarantine. However, your pet will have to be wormed
and treated for ticks by an approved vet in France 24-48
hours before re-entering Britain.

TAKING YOUR PET TO
GERMANY

If you want to take your pet with you to Germany and then bring him back into Great Britain at the end of your stay, you will have to do the following:

1. Get your pet microchipped.

2. Get your pet vaccinated against rabies.

3. Get your pet blood-sampled to show the rabies vaccination has worked. This sample will have to be taken 30 days after the vaccination.

If you do the above before April 2000, your pet will be able to travel immediately after April 2000.

If the above is done after April 2000, you will have to wait 6 months after the blood test before your pet will be eligible to travel.

4. Contact MAFF and request a bilingual rabies certificate for Germany.
MAFF
Animal Health (International Trade) Division B
Hook Rise South
Tolworth
Surbiton
Surrey KT6 7NT
Tel:- 020 8330 8184

5. Check that your vet is an appointed LVI (Local Veterinary Inspector.) If not, find one that is.
Get him or her to fill in and sign the bilingual certification of vaccination for rabies. The vaccination must have been given not less than 30 days – and not more than 12 months – before travelling.

6. No import permit is required provided:

a) the animal(s) are accompanied
b) There are no more than 3 animals even when accompanied
c) The animals are over 8 weeks old.
d) The animals are not for sale.

7. Check with your carrier – airline, ferry company etc – whether they require a health certificate saying the animal is fit to travel. Most do and this is issued privately by your vet.

8. Remember, if you are travelling through any other countries to reach Germany, you will have to fulfil each

TAKING YOUR PET TO GERMANY

country's import requirements.

BRINGING YOUR PET BACK FROM GERMANY

Provided you complied with the microchipping, rabies vaccination and blood-testing before you left, your pet will be allowed back into Britain without having to go into quarantine. However, your pet will have to be wormed and treated for ticks by an approved vet in Germany, 24-48 hours before re-entering Britain. Remember, if you travel through other countries, you will have to satisfy each country's import requirements. If, for instance, you go via France, you must have the necessary paperwork for importing a dog or cat into France, as well as for Germany. The worming and treatment for ticks may have to be done in France, depending on time spent in France, ferry times etc.

TAKING YOUR PET TO
ITALY

If you want to take your pet with you to Italy and then bring him or her back into Great Britain at the end of your stay, you will have to do the following:

1. Get your pet microchipped.

2. Get your pet vaccinated against rabies.

3. Get your pet blood-sampled to show the rabies vaccination has worked. This sample will have to be taken 30 days after the vaccination.

If you do the above before April 2000, your pet will be able to travel immediately after April 2000.

If the above is done after April 2000, you will have to wait 6 months after the blood test before your pet will be eligible to travel.

4. Contact
   MAFF
   Animal Health (International Trade) Division B
   Hook Rise South, Tolworth, Surbiton
   Surrey KT6 7NT
   Tel:- 020 8330 8184

Request the bilingual certificate for export of dogs and cats to Italy.

6. Check that your vet is an appointed LVI (Local Veterinary Inspector.) If not, find one that is.
Take the bilingual certificate to the LVI. Get him or her to complete and sign the form. This has to be done within 48 hours of travelling.

7. Remember, if you are going through another country, e.g. France, you will have to comply with the French regulations and have all the necessary paperwork.

BRINGING YOUR PET BACK FROM ITALY

Provided you complied with the microchipping, rabies vaccination and blood-testing before you left, your pet will be allowed back into Britain without having to go into quarantine. However, your pet will have to be wormed and treated for ticks by an approved vet in Italy 24-48 hours before re-entering Britain. Remember, if you travel through other countries you will have to satisfy each country's import requirements. If, for instance, you go via France, you will have to have the necessary paperwork for importing a dog or cat into France (see Page 38) as well as for Italy. The worming and treatment for ticks may have to be done in France, depending on time spent in France, ferry times etc.

TAKING YOUR PET TO
SPAIN

If you want to take your pet with you to Spain and then bring him or her back into Great Britain at the end of your stay, you will have to do the following:

1. Get your pet microchipped.

2. Get your pet vaccinated against rabies.

3. Get your pet blood-sampled to show the rabies vaccination has worked. This sample will have to be taken 30 days after the vaccination.

If you do the above before April 2000, your pet will be able to travel immediately after April 2000.

If the above is done after April 2000, you will have to wait 6 months after the blood test before your pet will be eligible to travel.

4. Contact
MAFF
Animal Health (International Trade) Division B
Hook Rise South
Tolworth
Surbiton
Surrey KT6 7NT
Tel:- 020 8330 8184

Request the bilingual certificate for export of dogs and cats to Spain. Also required is an owner's bilingual declaration, which you have to fill in and sign. This contains a declaration that you have owned the animal for the last 3 months or since birth; that the animal has not been imported; that the animal will be accompanied and that the animal will not be sold. This is, again, supplied by MAFF.

6. Check that your vet is an appointed LVI (Local Veterinary Inspector.) If not, find one that is.
Take the bilingual certificate to the LVI. Get him or her to complete and sign the form.
This must be done within 5 days of travelling.

8. Remember, if you are going through another country e.g. France, you will have to comply with the French regulations and have all the necessary paperwork.

9. Remember, the Canary Islands are included in the scheme but Ceuta and Melilla, the Spanish territories in North Africa, do not qualify for the Pet Travel Scheme.

BRINGING YOUR PET BACK FROM SPAIN

Provided you complied with the microchipping, rabies vaccination and blood-testing before you left, your pet will be allowed back into Britain without having to go into quarantine. However, your pet will have to be wormed and treated for ticks by an approved vet in Spain 24-48 hours before re-entering Britain. Remember, if you travel through other countries you will have to satisfy each country's import requirements. If, for instance, you go via France, you will have to have the necessary paperwork for importing a dog or cat into France, as well as for Spain. The worming and treatment for ticks may have to be done in France, depending on time spent in France, ferry times etc.

TAKING YOUR PET TO
BELGIUM

If you want to take your pet with you to Belgium and then bring him back into Great Britain at the end of your stay, you will have to do the following:

1. Get your pet microchipped.

2. Get your pet vaccinated against rabies.

3. Get your pet blood-sampled to show the rabies vaccination has worked. This sample will have to be taken 30 days after the vaccination.

If you do the above before April 2000, your pet will be able to travel immediately after April 2000.

If the above is done after April 2000, you will have to wait 6 months after the blood test before your pet will be eligible to travel.

4. Contact MAFF and request a bilingual rabies certificate
   for Belgium.
   MAFF
   Animal Health (International Trade) Division B
   Hook Rise South
   Tolworth
   Surbiton
   Surrey KT6 7NT
   Tel:- 020 8330 8184

5. Check that your vet is an appointed LVI (Local
   Veterinary Inspector.) If not, find one that is.
   Get him or her to fill in and sign the bilingual
   certification of vaccination for rabies. The
   vaccination must have been given not less than 30
   days and not more than 12 months before travelling.

6. Check with your carrier – airline, ferry company etc. –
   whether they require a health certificate saying the
   animal is fit to travel. Most do and this is issued
   privately by your vet.

7. Remember, if you are travelling through any other
   countries to reach Belgium, you will have to fulfil
   each country's import requirements.

BRINGING YOUR PET BACK FROM BELGIUM

Provided you complied with the microchipping, rabies
vaccination and blood-testing before you left, your pet
will be allowed back into Britain without having to go

into quarantine. However, your pet will have to be wormed and treated for ticks by an approved vet in Belgium, 24-48 hours before re-entering Britain. Remember, if you travel through other countries you will have to satisfy each country's import requirements. If, for instance, you go via France, you will need the necessary paperwork for importing a dog or cat into France, as well as for Belgium. The worming and treatment for ticks may have to be done in France, depending on time spent in France, ferry times etc.

FOREIGN
DISEASES

It may be worth considering insuring your pet against veterinary fees when on holiday. So far, only one insurance company, Pet Protect, is offering insurance cover for pets abroad. No doubt others will follow suit.

FOREIGN DISEASES

If you take your pet abroad, you should be aware of diseases seen there which are not normally seen in the UK. Most of these apply to dogs but some have also been recorded in cats.

Most of these diseases are spread by insects.

HEARTWORM

As the name suggests, this worm develops in the heart itself, on the valves. The larvae are present in the bloodstream, and are transmitted by a mosquito sucking the blood of an infected animal and then transferring this to a second animal. It takes about seven months to develop worms on the heart from the time of being bitten by an infected mosquito.

Many species of mosquito are capable of transferring the parasite, many of which already exist in southern England. As yet heartworm has only appeared in the UK in some imported animals.

TREATMENT

Once an animal has developed heartworm, the outlook is very grim. Killing the worms in the heart is easy enough but will result in a heart attack and death. As with most things, prevention is better than cure.

PREVENTION

Animals travelling to areas where heartworm occurs should go to a local vet on arrival and purchase heartworm tablets. These are given once a month while in the area.

AREAS AFFECTED

Heartworm is more prevalent in the southern areas, such as southern France, Spain, Italy and around the Mediterranean. There is a particularly high incidence in the Canary Islands.

BABESIOSIS

This bug causes damage to red blood cells, leading to anaemia and a whole range of symptoms such as red-coloured urine. The disease is often fatal or can leave the animal debilitated and prone to recurrent bouts of illness. The Babesiosis bug is spread by certain tick species found throughout Europe. The disease is particularly prevalent in France, especially south of the Loire valley.

PREVENTION

Proper treatment for ticks, e.g. Frontline, is vital in stopping infection from developing. If the ticks can be removed in the first day or so, infection can be prevented. It is worth checking through your pet's coat on a daily basis and removing any ticks.

EHRLICHOSIS

This is another disease spread by ticks. It causes vague signs of illness, often with a high temperature and swollen glands. Treatment with certain types of antibiotic early enough may be successful.

The disease is found particularly around the Mediterranean and also in the Rhone valley.

Again, prevention is aimed at removing or killing the ticks before they can infect your pet.

LEISHMANIASIS

This disease is characterised by recurring bouts of lethargy, weight loss, skin problems, kidney problems and others symptoms. Treatment is possible but care must be taken, as the disease can by caught by humans.

The disease is spread by sandflies and occurs around the Mediterranean, particularly in Sardinia and Sicily.

EMERGENCIES

HEAT STROKE

Dogs and cats sweat only through their pads and noses. To lose heat, they pant. By doing so, they also lose water, which evaporates from the respiratory tract. Heat stroke can occur very rapidly and not always on hot days.

CAUSES

Confinement in a poorly ventilated space, such as a car. Matters will be made worse if the car is in direct sunlight.

Excessive exercise can cause heat stroke. Dogs that love to play will often over-exercise to the point of heat exhaustion. Be aware of this, especially on hot days.

Lack of drinking water will lead to dehydration, especially in a dog that is panting.

Certain breeds with short noses – the Bulldog and Boxer, for instance (so-called brachiocephalic breeds) – are more prone to heat stroke.

Overweight pets are more prone to heat stroke.

SIGNS

Very fast panting, so fast it may be impossible to count – but the rate can be over 200 pants per minute.

Noisy/difficult breathing; rasping sounds not unlike somebody with asthma.

Salivation – the saliva may be very thick and sticky due to dehydration.

Staggering and lack of coordination. This is due to dehydration. If this persists unchecked, it will rapidly result in collapse.

Bright red gums. This is due to over oxygenation of the blood during panting. In near death cases, the gums may be blue or cyanotic. This is due to shock and circulatory collapse.

Rapid pulse. This is best felt in the animal's groin, but can be observed in smooth-coated animals by raising the head and observing just to one side of the windpipe.

High temperature. If a thermometer is available, the rectal temperature will be 105-110 degrees Fahrenheit/41-43 degrees Centigrade. Do not wait to confirm rectal temperature if heat stroke is suspected – start treatment immediately.

Other signs may include vomiting and/or diarrhoea.

TREATMENT

Remove from direct sun or confined space and move to a shaded area.

Start cooling the animal and contact a vet immediately.

Soak with water. Submerge in the sea, a river, pond or bath if possible. Hose or spray gently with water. Consider using packs of frozen vegetables as ice packs. These are particularly useful to apply around the head in attempt to cool the brain.

Provide fresh drinking water.

Take your animal to the vet. Even if signs start to improve, you should still take your pet to the vet as soon as possible. If signs fail to improve, the vet may have to put your animal on a drip and may even give a cold water enema.

PREVENTION

Do not leave animals in cars. Even in winter, the sun on a car window can turn the inside into an oven very quickly.

Avoid strenuous exercise and long walks on hot days. Consider taking your dog for a walk early in the morning or later in the evening.

Always have fresh water available.

Make your pet sit in the shade or confine him to the house on hot days.

Make sure your pet is the correct weight.

BEE AND WASP STINGS

Both dogs and cats will chase these, and sooner or later they get stung. Stings are usually on the lips or mouth, but can be on the head and feet. Unfortunately, dogs and cats do not seem to learn from their mistakes and will often still chase insects after a sting.

SIGNS

You may have seen your pet chasing a bee or wasp.

Pain. Your pet may yelp or cry out and then try to rub or scratch at the affected area.

Swelling. The local area may become very swollen very quickly.

Salivation. If the sting is in the mouth or lips, this is a common sign.

It is sometimes possible to see a sting.

TREATMENT

Look for a sting and remove carefully, preferably with tweezers. (This prevents further venom being squeezed out of the sting and into your animal.)

Apply an ice pack to the area to reduce swelling and to localise the spread of the sting.

If the sting is to the head or lips, or if the swelling is great, contact a vet. Some stings, especially around the face, can also cause swelling of the larynx, which can block the windpipe.

JELLYFISH STINGS

Dogs swimming in the sea are just as likely to be stung by jellyfish as people, if not more so.

SIGNS

Pain around the area. Your dog may be chewing, licking or scratching at the area. There may be a jellyfish tentacle caught in your dog's coat.

TREATMENT

Remove the tentacle, taking care not to sting yourself. Use rubber gloves if possible or improvise and use a plastic bag or poop scoop bag.

Wash the area in fresh water and apply ice if available.

Seek veterinary attention if your dog seems in distress.

TICKS

If you take your pet to rural areas, both in this country and abroad, you are likely to come across ticks. These creatures live in hedgerows, woodland and long grass. They are usually grey or cream in colour. They only feed for several days once a year. They hop on a passing host (this may be your pet or even yourself!) and sink their mouth parts through the skin and suck blood. They attach themselves strongly and, if left, will suck blood for up to 12 days. As they do so, their bodies swell. If your pet has a tick, it is not possible for you to catch the same tick from your pet, but it is possible for you to pick up a tick from the same location as your pet.

SIGNS

Irritation at site. Your pet may gnaw or scratch around the area.

May be found incidentally when brushing or patting.

TREATMENT

Ticks are best removed as soon as possible. It is important to remove the tick in its entirety. A local reaction or even abscess may form if the mouth parts are left behind. Do not be tempted to use lighted cigarettes or other crude methods. Do not just pull at the body, but grasp the whole tick as close to your pet's skin as possible and gently twist. Simple tick removers which lever the head parts out are available from pet shops.

PREVENTION

It is impossible to prevent your pet from picking up ticks if you are in a tick area. Many flea treatments claim to kill ticks, but this is often only true if the medication is applied directly onto the tick. The exception to this is Frontline (Merial) which is only available from your vet.

Ticks should be removed immediately they are found. They can carry Lyme's disease, which affects both people and animals. The bug which causes Lyme's disease (*Boriella burgdorfii*) is carried on the mouth parts of the tick but only passes to the host (you or your pet) after 24 hours. Therefore, it is important to remove the tick within the first 24 hours. Lyme's disease occurs only sporadically in the UK at the moment but may become more widespread.

The advice then is to check through your pet's coat regularly and remove any ticks immediately. If in any doubt, contact a vet.

TICK LIFE CYCLE

The tick's life cycle can range from a few months to two years. Each developmental stage of a tick's life requires a blood meal in order to reach the next stage. Some species can survive for years without feeding.

SNAKE BITE

The UK has only one poisonous snake, the adder, which is not uncommon in the southern half of the country, particularly around the New Forest area in Hampshire. However, in Europe, USA and Australia there are many more species.

SIGNS

Often the owner will not see the dog being bitten. The bite usually happens when a dog disturbs a snake in undergrowth.

Pain. There will be intense pain at the bite site. If bitten on a leg, the dog may carry the leg. Biting or licking at an area may indicate the site. Look for two small red marks close together, made by the fangs.

Swelling. Snakebites usually swell very quickly.

Other signs. One or all of these other signs may also be present.
• Trembling.

• Rapid pulse.
• Collapse.

TREATMENT

Prevent excess movement, which will spread the venom further. Often a dog bitten by a snake will be very scared and may try to run off.

Restrain your dog if necessary.

Lightly grip above the bite, but not so hard as to restrict blood flow.

Apply an ice pack if available.

Seek veterinary attention immediately.

Snake bites cause constriction of blood vessels which can mean a shutting off of blood supply to the affected area. This can lead to that area going gangrenous or can even lead to death.

DROWNING

Most dogs and cats can swim, but drowning incidents do occur. Examples are when dogs become fatigued; fall into steep-sided places, such as swimming pools or canals; fall into fast-running rivers where their swimming skills are little use; or fall through ice.

Do not put yourself at risk. Remember your dog will be panicking and may drag you down with him.

Attempt to rescue your dog from dry land or a boat.

Try to hook him by the collar.

If you do decide to enter the water, take something the dog can cling to, such as a float or an inflatable airbed.

Get the dog ashore. If he is conscious, keep him quiet and warm. Give some form of energy food, such as a sweet biscuit.

If your dog is unconscious, suspend him or her by the back legs (as shown below) to drain water from the lungs.

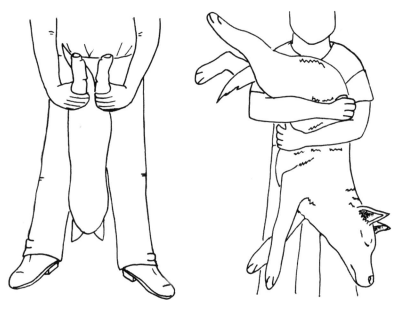

If your dog is a large breed, pick him or her up around the chest and gently squeeze.

ARTIFICIAL RESPIRATION

Lay your dog on his or her side.
Grab the tongue and pull forward.
Clear the mouth and back of the throat of any debris or saliva.

Close your dog's mouth and hold shut with your left hand. Make a loose fist with your right hand. Place your 4th and 5th fingers around your dog's nostrils. Place your lips over your thumb and index finger and blow, as shown below.

You should see your dog's chest rise. Release your lips and you should see the chest fall. Repeat at 10-second intervals.

If there is no response after 1 or 2 breaths, check for a heartbeat. This is best felt under the front leg close to the elbow, with the dog on his or her side.
If a beat is felt, continue artificial respiration.

CARDIAC MASSAGE

If no heartbeat is felt, push firmly and briskly with the palm of your hand on your dog's chest, just behind where the elbow lies.

Do half a dozen compressions in quick succession and then give two breaths by artificial respiration. Repeat the compressions until a heartbeat is felt or the dog starts to breathe. Seek veterinary advice immediately.

ROAD TRAFFIC ACCIDENT

Car accidents involving dogs and cats are all too common.

Injuries can range from minor cuts and grazes to massive internal damage and death.

If your animal is involved in an RTA (road traffic accident), approach the situation in the following manner.

Don't panic.
Restrain your animal. Your animal will be scared and even dazed. He may not recognise or respond to you. An animal's natural instinct is to run and go to ground. Try to get an injured cat into a basket or box. Make this more appealing by blacking out the side. A laundry basket will suffice in an emergency.

Your animal may be in great pain and may attempt to bite. You may have to muzzle your dog. A necktie or pair of tights makes an adequate muzzle.

Remove your pet from the road. In human medicine, where an ambulance will come to the victims, you are taught not to move an injured person. No such emergency system exists for animals, and your pet will have to be moved at some point to a vet's surgery. Use a blanket or towel as a stretcher.

For cats, try wrapping a large towel around them and then transfer them to a basket or other carrier.

If your animal is not breathing, follow the procedure for artificial respiration (Page 65).

If there is no heartbeat, follow the procedure for cardiac massage (Page 66) but be careful – there may be fractured ribs or other injuries which may be made worse by rough handling of the chest.

Take to a vet immediately.

BLEEDING

Major external bleeding will be obvious. Apply compression to the area using a towel, shirt or other piece of material. Do not worry about infection at this stage. Do not dab the blood away but keep constant pressure on the bleeding area.

Take to a vet immediately.

CUTS AND GRAZES

Some cuts bleed profusely, even from the smallest of wounds. Again, the crucial thing here is to apply pressure. Get some sort of material – a handkerchief or T-shirt, cotton wool if you have it – and wrap it around the bleeding area. Apply direct pressure with your thumb if necessary. The temporary bandage can be held in place with sticky tape or even tied on with string.

If there is a wound to the head or ear, use cut-off tights to make a tube to hold the padding in place.

Seek veterinary attention immediately.

VOMITING

A lot of animals are sick when travelling. In most cases, it's just a question of clearing up the mess and following the advice earlier in the book in an attempt to prevent this in the future.

However, if your pet continues vomiting then there may be another cause.

If you pet is being sick, withhold food.

Offer small amounts of fresh water often – about every hour. Do not offer large amounts to a vomiting animal as they may drink a whole bellyful and then just throw the lot back up. If possible, offer cooled boiled water. Any chlorine in the water which your pet, with a keener sense of smell, may detect, will be removed by the boiling.

If your pet is dull, showing signs of pain or discomfort, or the vomit contains blood or what looks like brown coffee grains, seek veterinary advice immediately

If your pet is bright and alert with no sign of pain, continue to offer small amounts of water. After about 12 hours, try a light diet such as scrambled egg, chicken, fish or plain boiled white rice. Do not offer too much at one meal – split the ration into a number of smaller meals.

If the vomiting recurs, or if your pet becomes dull or refuses food, seek veterinary attention.

BLOAT/GASTRIC DILATATION/TORSION

Bloat is usually seen in large deep-chested dogs such as German Shepherd Dogs, Mastiffs, Newfoundlands and Irish Setters, and is a real emergency. A Staffordshire Bull Terrier is the smallest dog I have ever seen with this condition.

The condition is seen a few hours after feeding. Often there will have been a change to the normal routine – maybe a change of food or time of feeding.

The dog becomes increasingly distressed and may attempt to vomit.

The stomach will start to swell and distend, and, if tapped, will sound like a drum.

Breathing will become rapid and shallow.

The mucus membranes may be pale or very congested.

Seek veterinary attention immediately. Even with the correct, prompt attention, this condition is often fatal, and early recognition and treatment are vital.

In this condition the stomach fills with gas, and puts pressure on the lungs and vessels returning blood to the heart. The dog rapidly goes into shock. Bacteria and toxins inside the stomach begin to get into the bloodstream, making matters worse. If this distention is not relieved then the stomach twists (rather like trying to hold an inflated balloon down under water; eventually it twists to one side and rises). The blood supply to the stomach is then shut off, and very quickly the stomach will rupture and the dog will die.

APPENDIX 1

USEFUL NUMBERS: OFFICIAL BODIES

PETS (Pet Travel Scheme)
Helpline:- 020 8330 6835

Passports For Pets
20 Seymour Road
London
SW18 5JA
Tel:- 020 8870 5960

Ministry of Agriculture, Fisheries
and Food (MAFF)
Hook Rise South
Tolworth
Surbiton
Surrey
KT6 7HF
Tel:-0181 330 4411
Helpline:- 0645 335577
www.maff.gov.uk/animalh/
quarantine/default.htm

Royal College of Veterinary
Surgeons
Belgravia House
62-62 Horseferry Road
London
SW1P 2AF
Tel:- 020 7222 2001

British Veterinary Association
7 Mansfield Street
London
W1M 0AT
Tel:- 020 7636 6541

British Small Animal Veterinary
Association
1 Telford Way
Waterwells Business Park
Quedgeley
Gloucester
GL2 4AB
Tel:- 01452 726700

APPENDIX 2

USEFUL PRODUCTS AND SERVICES

PET SITTERS
Animal Angels
Tel:- 01256 764141

Animal Aunts
Tel:- 01730 821529

The Home Service
Tel:- 0800 0746642

Homesitters
Tel:- 01296 630730

Minders Keepers
Tel:- 01763 262102

Pet Lodgers
Tel:- 020 8786 7215

The Sitting Service
Tel:- 01422 368692

Stay Safe Sitters
Tel:- 01225 851288

PET INSURANCE ABROAD
Pet Protect
55 High Street
Epsom
Surrey
KT19 8PP
Tel:- 0800 650 056

AIRLINE APPROVED TRANSPORTERS/CRATES

Air Pets Oceanic
Willowslea Farm Kennels
Stanwellmore
Nr Staines
Middlesex
Tel:- 01753 685571

Stock Nutrition
Station Road
Yaxham
Norfolk
NR19 1RD
Tel:- 01362 694957

Oakenshaw Grange
Doncaster Road
Crofton
Wakefield
West Yorkshire
WF4 1SD
Tel:- 01924 863795

PET EXPORT SPECIALISTS
See Air Pets Oceanic above

LIFE JACKETS FOR DOGS

Nauticalia Maritime Mail Order
Catalogue
The Ferry point
Ferry Lane
Shepperton-on-Thames
TW17 9QL
Tel:- 01932 253333
www.nauticalia.co.uk

Craftsafe Marketing Ltd
Unit 4
Mitchell Point
Ensign Business Park
Hamble
Southampton
SO31 4RF
Tel:- 01703 454272

TRAVELLING PRODUCTS

Instinctively Cats and Dogs
The Seedbed Centre
Langston Road
Loughton
Essex
IG10 3TQ
Tel:- 020 8502 4487
www.incatdog.com

Ventilex Products Ltd
PO Box 241
Chesham
Bucks
HP5 3SB
Tel:- 01494 784245

INDEX

A

abroad, 27
acepromazine, 19
ACP, 19
Adder, 62
airbed, 64
airlines, 27
anti emetic, 19
Artificial Respiration, 65
Australia, 33

B

Babesiosis, 53
Bees, 58
Belgium, 51
bilingual certificate, 39, 45, 47
Bleeding, 69
blinds, 18
Bloat, 71
blood test, 36
blood-tested, 35
Boat, 25
booster, 13
boosters, 13
Boriella burgdorfii, 61
bowls, 15
Brucellosis, 33

C

Cages, 28
Canal Boats, 25
Canary Islands, 47
Car travel, 17
Cardiac Massage, 66

H

I

J

K

L

M

T

U

V

W

Y